Days out in Summer

Vic Parker

Heinemann
LIBRARY

Little Nippers

www.heinemann.co.uk/library
Visit our website to find out more information about **Heinemann Library** books.

To order:
☎ Phone 44 (0) 1865 888066
▤ Send a fax to 44 (0) 1865 314091
▣ Visit the Heinemann Bookshop at www.heinemann.co.uk/library to browse our catalogue and order online.

First published in Great Britain by Heinemann Library, Halley Court, Jordan Hill, Oxford OX2 8EJ, part of Harcourt Education. Heinemann is a registered trademark of Harcourt Education Ltd.

Editorial: Jilly Attwood and Claire Throp
Design: Jo Hinton-Malivoire and bigtop, Bicester, UK
Models made by: Jo Brooker
Picture Research: Rosie Garai, Sally Smith and Debra Weatherley
Production: Séverine Ribierre

Originated by Dot Gradations
Printed and bound in China by South China Printing Company

ISBN 978 0 431 17302 3 (hardback)
08 07 06 05 04
10 9 8 7 6 5 4 3 2 1

ISBN 978 0 431 17307 8 (paperback)
09 08
10 9 8 7 6 5 4 3

British Library Cataloguing in Publication Data
Parker, Vic
Days out in summer
508.2
A full catalogue record for this book is available from the British Library.

Acknowledgements
The publisher would like to thank the following for permission to reproduce photographs: Alamy/Robert Harding Picture Library p. **12–13**; Bubbles pp. **16–17** (Angela Hampton), **22** (Ian West); Corbis p. **10–11** (Michael Keller), p. **11 top**; KPT Power Photos p. **17 top**; Masterfile p. **19** (Ariel Skelley); Peter Evans p. **6**; Photofusion p. **21** (Stephen Coyne); Robert Harding Picture Library pp. **7** (Jane Legate), **23** (Mula Eshet); Science Photo Library pp. **4** (David Parker), **15** (Ron Sutherland); Steve Behr/Stockfile p. **18**; Trip p. **20** (J. Garrett); Tudor Photography p. **8–9**.

Cover photograph reproduced with permission of Getty Images/Philip & Karen Smith.

The publishers would like to thank Annie Davy for her assistance in the preparation of this book.

Every effort has been made to contact copyright holders of any material reproduced in this book. Any omissions will be rectified in subsequent printings if notice is given to the publishers.

The paper used to print this book comes from sustainable resources.

Contents

It's summertime!

Summer is the **hottest** time of the year.

Play at the park

What do you like best at the park?

Hold on tight!

Splash time

A perfect way of keeping **cool** is splashing about in a paddling pool.

9

Fun in the fields

Summer grass is tall and tickly!

11

Carnival time

There's a **party** in the street.

Enjoy the carnival!

On the sand

A day at the beach.

Don't forget your suncream

At the sea shore

Do you like jumping the waves?

What shape
are these sea
creatures?

Picnic treat

No need to stay indoors for meals in summer.

Fun in the sun!

Pack a picnic instead.

Boating trip

At the lake you can float your toy boat.

Keeping cool

When the sunshine gets too **hot**, make a **shady** den.

Or **cool** off with a tasty ice-cream. Yum!

Index

The end

Notes for adults

The *Days out in...* series helps young children become familiar with the way their environment changes through the year. The books explore the natural world in each season and how this affects community life and social activities. Used together, the books will enable discussion about similarities and differences between the seasons, how the natural world follows a cyclical pattern, and how different people mark special dates in the year. The following Early Learning Goals are relevant to this series:

Knowledge and understanding of the world

Early learning goals for exploration and investigation
• look closely at similarities, differences, patterns and change.

Early learning goals for sense of time
• observe changes in the environment, for example through the seasons.

Early learning goals for cultures and beliefs
• begin to know about their own cultures and beliefs and those of other people.

This book introduces the reader to the season of summer. It will encourage young children to think about summer weather, wildlife and landscape; activities they can enjoy in summer; and what clothes it is appropriate to wear. The book will help children extend their vocabulary, as they will hear new words such as *carnival* and *suncream*. You may like to introduce and explain other new words yourself, such as *costume* and *tide*.

Additional information about the seasons

Not all places in the world have four seasons. Climate is affected by two factors: 1) how near a place is to the Equator (hence how much heat it receives from the Sun), 2) how high a place is (mountains are cooler than nearby lowlands). This is why some parts of the world have just two seasons, such as the hot wet season and the hot dry season across much of India. Other parts of the world have just one season, such as the year-long heat of the Sahara desert or the year-long cold of the North Pole.

Follow-up activities

• Collect some feathers, ribbons and sequins and make a bright carnival head-dress.
• Make some tasty homemade ice-cream.
• Pack up a picnic lunch to enjoy in the garden or park – or indoors!

Little Nippers

Days out in

Summer

Days out in investigates the *seasons* by exploring various activities that children may take part in. Each title also looks at what clothes you might wear, what the weather is like, and other changes in the environment. The series provides an excellent opportunity for discussing similarities, differences and patterns between seasons, the way these changes affect social activities, and the child's own experiences and feelings.

Little Nippers

Little Nippers is a collection of information books designed to support the Curriculum Guidance for the Foundation Stage.
The series in *Little Nippers* cover a wide range of topics allowing children to gain knowledge and understanding of the world around them. These non-fiction books have a playful, unpredictable approach to maintain children's interest. Open-ended questions provide opportunities for interaction and discussion with children, while variation in text and design provides greater flexibility of use for the books.

Features in **Little Nippers** include:
· playful designs to attract attention
· clear, high-quality photographs to stimulate discussion
· notes for adults with suggestions on how to use the book and additional
  information for answering children's questions
· non-fiction book features such as a contents page, page numbers and index.

Titles in **Days out in** include:

These books are also available in a hardback edition.

Find out about the full range of Heinemann Library
resources at **www.heinemann.co.uk/library**

The Little Nippers crab and friends appear throughout the series so have fun finding them!

Heinemann
LIBRARY

ISBN 978-0-431-17307-8

9 780431 173078

£ 5.99